# Chalk Poets

WINCHESTER
**POETRY**
FESTIVAL

SOUTH DOWNS
NATIONAL PARK

# Chalk Poets
## New poetry from the South Downs

Edited by Stephanie Norgate

Winchester Poetry Festival

First published 2016 by Winchester Poetry Festival
41 Nuns Road, Winchester SO23 7EF

Poems copyright © individual authors 2016 unless otherwise stated
Introduction copyright © Stephanie Norgate 2016

## Acknowledgements

With grateful appreciation to South Downs National Park Authority for financial assistance towards this publication and also towards the commissioning of seven new poems about the South Downs: 'Ice' by Hannah Brockbank, 'The Chalk Dragon' by Lydia Fulleylove, 'A Piece of Chalk' by Kate Miller, 'The Strange Children' by Zoe Mitchell, 'Daedalus over the Downs' by Stephanie Norgate, 'Highdown' by Steven O'Brien, 'Get Thee Glass Eyes' by Colette Sensier.

Thanks to Greenwich Exchange for permission to include 'Wild Hunt' and 'Zither Child', from *Scrying Stone* by Steven O'Brien.

Thanks to Eyewear Press for permission to include 'In the Weald' and 'Marguerite' from *Skinless* by Colette Sensier.

## Cover Illustration

'Chalk Paths' by Eric Ravilious, courtesy of Bridgeman Images
Chalk Paths, Ravilious, Eric (1903 42) / Private Collection / Bridgeman Images

Designed by Andy Key andy@freewheel.org.uk
Printed by Sarsen Press www.sarsenpress.co.uk

# Contents

# Introduction

I have walked the South Downs all my life, and so the invitation to edit this anthology and to curate the Chalk Poets' reading was very welcome. The South Downs National Park area is, perhaps not surprisingly, home to many fine poets. Inevitably I could only include a few of them – a mix of the experienced and the new – and so apologies to the many others who would have also made interesting contributions.

To walk the Downs is to face both natural beauty and a certain harshness. There are sunny banks of cowslips imbued with that particular chalk land scent and the song of skylarks hovering, but on a different kind of day, the walker can find themselves tramping through messenger clouds with their low chilling damp, past burial grounds and through slithers of mud.

To walk the Downs is to face something in yourself too, as you glimpse the very edge of our country in the distance, with the Channel marking our separation from others. One of my regular walks takes me past a memorial stone for a German pilot shot down in World War II. Locals hang poppies in the overhead branches and pile them on to the stone, sudden red shocks against the black-green cave of the copse. Even the most magical landscape can never be escapist, but is marked by the losses of history and by human activity.

The poets published here face the making and breaking of relationships, their adventuring selves and the otherness of nature, all embedded in the chalky ridges and scars of the downland. There are references to previous literary walkers of the Downs, Edward Thomas and G K Chesterton, to mythic creatures, fabled children, bell barrows and buried daggers, insects and flowers, broken farm machinery and domestic dissonance, teenagers on the cusp of adulthood, hiking gear, paragliding, artistic practice, and to metaphysical and uncanny visions. Private and public pasts merge in this meditative walking and composing on the Downs.

Thanks to South Downs National Park Authority for commissioning one new poem from each of us. The theme was so appealing that, out of the twenty-one poems published here, all but four are new and written expressly for the anthology.

Many thanks to my fellow contributors, Hannah Brockbank, Lydia Fulleylove, Kate Miller, Zoe Mitchell, Steven O'Brien and Colette Sensier for their intensely observed and powerful poems. I hope readers sense the downland with all its paradoxes and mysteries, and perhaps, after reading, will want to pull on their hiking boots and find a slanting white track up a hill.

*Stephanie Norgate*

# Hannah Brockbank

## Ice

### I

I remember the time
you said I was cold as ice.

I ran until I couldn't hear
the car's engine turn over,
or your heated calls rise up
over the downland.

I ran until I could hear
the grate of chalk
and the splosh of my boots
as the path turned white
and filled the deer tracks
with milky water,
and when I stopped,
I knelt down
and let it
wash over me.

### II

Ahead, a pale green globe
of chalk glows in the dusk;
a full stop in the path
              between
the firs and the field;
              between
    then and now.

Now, I see
how rain and frost
can prise stone          apart.
I trail my fingers
over the chalk's pitted surface,
poke my fingers through
the ice to feel
spined beech husks
and pine bark mouldering
underneath.

# Smallholding

Who upturned
the tractor behind the yew
and smashed saucers
against its rusted ribs?

Who snapped
the forget-me-not blue handle
off the chamber pot?

Who drained
the tincture bottles of remedies
and hurled them
onto the root strangled soil,
until the earth yielded
only shoots of green glass
as pitiless as the spike
piercing the sole
of my boot?

# By the Winterbourne

It claimed the path
and left us to teeter
along its silted edge.

Grass blades plastered
the toes of our boots
as we avoided the tangle
of water speedwell,
sweet grass and starwort.

Higher up the path,
you worked your hand loose
from mine and pointed
a stubby pink finger,
scoured raw by the wind,
towards a chalk ball
turning over in the silt.
You dipped down
and caught it.

The white globe
nestled in your palm
like an unhatched egg.

# Lydia Fulleylove

## *The Chalk Dragon*

whose wings are fledgling    sketched in
whose short tail sprung       as if for flight

makes out himself

not the jaunt of a chalk horse

but a trace of chalk
a scraped white line of thought

he contemplates ascent
watches clouds    like chalk rubbings in the sky

the discs of a dragon's tail   in a tapering curve of vapour

which the wind smudges

he brushes scrabbly grass
wild thyme and white snail shells

he rides the ridges like green waves
he leaves himself behind

a sleep or sense print
which sheep now press against and hollow out

# *The Path to the Combe*

Not a chalk hill blue, but an orange tip
settling on a ferny leaf of Queen Anne's lace,
flickering up to sketch fine lines of flight,

the path streaking whiter as we climb, lighter,
brighter, stumbling from the holloway
to knobbled stones and scattered flints and roots

dusted white, like dry gnarled bones, its skin
thinning as it rises onto the down's flank
where chalk breaks through the green, the air tipping

into blue above the ridge, daisies speckling
white as if sky-fallen flowers
and a chalk hill blue, its wings chalk-etched, shuts

its flight a second to camouflage in grey
against the path.  We hesitate –
whether to take the white track cut between the banks

or scramble up the shoulder of the combe
tumbling the chalk, skimming the rim above
the elder, hawthorn, tangled brambles

to balance on a thin lid of brown earth  —

# *Descent*

the rim of the combe
the toes of our boots
the whiff of crushed marjoram
whitethroats and windsong

    the path slips away

a curve through wet grass
a white hyphen flash
in – out – of its sleeve of woods
vanishing under the dark
hood of hawthorn

    and look

the back of yourself walking down
blue top, rucksack, bare calves,
boots gripping the slither of chalk
the shine of the roots

    till you're gone

into a shuffling of seasons, weathers and years
the blackthorn, the hawthorn, the elder

    the rim of the combe

the whiff of crushed marjoram
whitethroats and windsong

# Kate Miller

## A Piece of Chalk

*But though I could not with a crayon get the best out of*
*the landscape, it does not follow that the landscape was*
*not getting the best out of me.*
               G K Chesterton, 'A Piece of Chalk'

I've been wanting to go on the Downs
to follow Chesterton

setting off, *one splendid morning blue and silver,*
his pocket stuffed with coloured chalks,
a pocket knife he called his *infant sword*
and papoose of brown parcel paper from the kitchen drawer.

He was happy with its rough-and-readiness: brownness was
*primeval* or *poetical,* a raw material
suited to the new day of creation,
with its yeasty odour of October woods or beer.

*Do not imagine,* he warned, *I was going to sketch*
*from Nature.* He was on a quest for mystical,
heraldic and symbolic beasts, *old gods*, a fiery flock of stars.

The first he drew in purple was a regal animal,
she shone with seven horns:
he saw her soul and mystery.

I'm wanting visions too. No ordinary
cow should be allowed to take my eye.
This isn't about scenery
except a glimpse perhaps – a pale green sea, the crowns
of far off trees – oceanic and processional.

I mean to cross *the swell of living turf,*
be granted what the downland
granted him, its queenly sweep of air and earth and light.

I want the pomp and glory of that loft
above the chalk, a whitening space, the place
you feel the power whiteness has
when white outdoes and gathers
force and leaps

away from earthy coloured things, out, up —
in crests, bubbles, traces, glints — white burning
haloes at the edge of dust in sunlight,
on leaves of grass, on ruts,
arcing off the filaments of harebells...

I'll reach the skyline, kneel
where a layer of thin soil's scraped,

maybe on the knoll where Chesterton had stopped
to find that he'd forgotten his white chalk.

Yet, this essential wanting, he was blessed
for it seemed boundless
white rose up, surrounded him and stretched
cloudlike, basilican,
aisle after aisle, rack upon rack – *an immense warehouse* of white

and with the penknife it was soft enough to cut
a piece to use, a piece of hill,

to dash in lights and heighten shapes and patches
on his page, render luminous and full
fantastical creations.

I like his rapt surprise about the way the mineral
in his hand had come to light
from underground, his sense the landscape worked
on him and not the other way around,

– that's what I've been wanting. To be subject
to the underlying chalk, accept its hold
on water, affinity with clouds,
waves, moon and bones,

accept the almost tidal pull
that brings me to a place on the South Downs
where I am one small pair of hands and knees,

one bowing pilgrim at a teeming shrine. Hoping to pass
unseen I'll kneel and prise a little bit of rock.

# Drawing in the Royal Hunting Wood

The paper is the forest's own
sweet chestnut, coppiced,
pulped: a factory roll
of ordinary brown.
I pat a long sheet
smooth on leaf mould,
buff beneath the trees'
green soffits.
My drawing floor's
marked out by flints
turned up when
charcoal burners
built a kiln.
I set out
tools: charcoal
sticks and foraged
lumps of dampish chalk.
At my back an apse of yew;
sun shuttles
in the warp of spider webs
        when a doe
        vaults
   off the forest path,
peppers the glade
with dots, gold
legs, fur, the flare of her
white scut.
Hoof marks patter
denting down
the length of paper,
laid like Raleigh's cape.
She veers away
and out to bracken,
leaving behind
her page.

# Another Almanac

### I

A child knows the joust of white
from living by the sea, familiar with the field
of water, the grand parade of plumes
and how mercurial it is: a long held tilt of tide
might climax in a criss-cross
clash of streaks or pass
with a mere glance.

Early on, she learned to read
the weather's tell-tales,
recognise white whisks, the blows –
sharp touch, blunt thwack – dealt by
an agile wind in swordplay.

A pearly coat of haze
she knows, conceals festivals.
One moment nothing's happening out there,
all's blank – the next, a crowd of showy
clouds musters and streams off
to promenade.

Sky above the sea's a city
charged with daily pageantry,
changing rhythms, changing light.

### II

But there's another country. Inland,
where she's sent to school,
a dash of white is rare. Chalk, flint, blossom,
bones and little snows appear
but not as she has known white, the view alive with
flecky short hand. She misses gusts on water,

gulls' scribble,
underlines of wakes.

Head bowed, she scours
brown paths for spots of lightness,
picking in wet shoes through woods and hangers
collaged in adhesive leaves
on ancient tracks where Edward Thomas loped
and often fell in step, he wrote,
with world-shy men who walked and kept
the paths open.

If time had been erased
and they had met, she might have asked
for help with names: pale moths,
slips of lint with dusty dots across the wing,
blurred as though a signature has run.
Or these? Doughy mushrooms
laid out under trees, funnels scented
like fresh flour, cloud-coloured, old ones
spreading into flattened saddles.

So much is underfoot, or unseen in the air,
on shelves of smell and sound
material and close.

III

Turning to books,
she opens in the quiet lichened library
another almanac
to chart the slower year of growth,
and settles after dark (beside a globe)
to read the earth and sky
in older poets' words.

# Zoe Mitchell

## The Strange Children

We all heard about the strange children
seized by the South Downs one hot summer.

They had been shepherds in their former home,
a place set between the dog and the wolf

where all light had departed and darkness
not yet descended. They lived in the lap

of expectant twilight until distant music
beckoned through an echo of caves, swinging

a bell of mystery. They stumbled out,
all work forgotten, a herd of lost beasts

trampling over the dry green of old hills
in August, blinking at a world made new.

Summer assaulted their senses at first –
they rubbed their eyes, felt heat prick their skin.

Their ears had been fine-tuned to the warning
held in coming darkness; they cowered

at the clamour of nature until the symphony
enchanted them; they heard each insect tick,

each feather ruffle. They heard each bee buzz
as they gulped pollen grains, gathering gold.

Each new sight they encountered was haloed,
every animal, plant and bird ringed with light.

The black silhouette of words had no place
in the grey land they came from; they had no

names for anything. The day waned. They rested
in a hollow, pale faces tipped to the sky.

Here they stayed, snared by the season, saying
nothing. Autumn's breath fell sour on them,

they were afraid and searched for their lost home.
A chill wind settled over them, frost grew beneath

and they wept, afraid their eyes had eaten
summer. They gathered in a chalk pit,

and their lungs wheezed shallow gasps of air.
They curled their small bodies into the crevasses

and waited for their white bones to crumble
into the foundations of a lost heaven.

# *As I Like It*

Far from jealous city windows, I'm safe –
away from everything but the weather.
The recurring nag of the winter's wind
wraps tight around my body in exile.

I ease into this one honest embrace.
Reduced now to a numb ice-element,
I move against invisible pressure,
find myself a place, draw myself closer.

The sucking mud roots me far from people.
The river scores its stories on the land
and they rise as whispers in the branches,
settle as lessons on the weathered rocks.

My heart may ghost a presence here, may shine
and illuminate. I would not change it.

# *Seven Sisters*

I came to these hills with a man I loved
once. He strode ahead, peered over cliff tops;

I hung back and tried to admire the view
from where I stood, but it still made me dizzy.

We wandered over crumbling peaks, trying
to make something of the last autumn sunshine.

I couldn't hide how the incline made me sweat;
I remember heat in my lungs, failing

to keep up, walking ahead when he stopped,
waiting for him to overtake me again.

I knew that these hills would be my home
and I must let him go, let salt water

eat through porous chalk and bear an eighth sister
in the constant rasping lap of the sea.

I stand there still, one more unwanted woman.

# Stephanie Norgate

## Daedalus over the Downs

A man puts his arm through the harness of his wing,
snaps the buckles fast, takes the weight of canvas,
and hears the baffled slings sing in his creaking ear.

Helmeted, he edges his way slope-wards,
breathing in the old chalkland scent. Over there where
the stunted families of hawthorn point wind-bitten arms
to the air, he runs down the curve as children do,
harum-scarum, running to fly.

He is a father, a new husband, then he's eighteen again,
his back against the vetch and creeping thistle,
a lovely girl warm beside him on the crushed thyme.
If only he could stop there, but he can't, he's fifteen
sitting on a log, smoking a secret spliff, he is ten weeping
for his dead dog, his only friend, and then his feet slip on chalk,
skid him into the launch.
      Now the arc of fabric fills
with air. So often he's wanted to ride a current
that will carry him to a truer view of the Downs.
White scars of paths drawn by foot or hoof
jitter towards him, juggling the scarps
then hiding themselves in the copse's caverns of yew.
And, gliding on, he catches the signal glints
from troughs, drenched coffins, man-sized baths,
that flash back his red half-moon on mirror
water. And, up over again where Didling church
marks the lane, the green corrugations
of barn roofs ripple away from him. Yellow fields
slant up to patch the lines below.
He's swearing with relief,

laughing now, talking to the air, to the skylarks,
as he sees his shadow wing skimming the blackthorn,
caressing the view in a way that he never could,
when he'd trailed his childhood hands over the scarp
and pressed his fingers into every valley of plaster
on the dusty contour map in the village hall.

Though his eyes water in the wind,
surely he has the measure of it now,
the Devil's Jumps humping their bell barrows
over the earth, their ancient burrowings.
But it was nothing like this, he thinks, nothing
like riding thermals, so far up that he can't
see the golden mouths of the buttercups
or, below him on the path, the ragged feather,
which has floated down, as his son's feather did,
to the white chalk beneath his dangling feet.

# The Other Side of the Downs

A cold June evening. Our grown children
newly gone again to their cities.

Up here, a pair of nesting jays lose their shyness,
flit in and out of the hawthorn's tunnel.

A buzzard puzzles the copse with wary turnings,
fogged by shreds of whirling smoke.

I want to know whether the blue-grey streak
on the other side is really the Channel,

a cloud hedge or a passing bruise of weather,
and why the stile must be a cross of steps,

and why the airy wire fences need to fence
the rattle of the seeding cowslips.

I need landmarks like this metal trough, where
sheep lap up the changing heavens.

I want to skip the scudding mist,
the slippery steep, and lark up and over

in a hover to a singing sky.
But I can't. And so this post, a star

of signs planted in its cairn of stones
may as well be my guide

to restricted bridleways, permitted footpaths
I follow the finger pointing

to that fenceless unnecessary gate
alone on the scarp's edge.

On the other side, a slope of orchids, darkly splashed,
falls away from the chalk scarred view.

No need for barriers on these open hills,
but someone's set a gate among the nettles.

And, though we could so freely go around
or over, something forces us through.

# *Under a Downland Tree*

to be shade pooling under a tree
a dark oval cast by the canopy
to write in the shade of this tree
to write in the shade of this tree

with the sheep and the rooks
and their prospecting looks
in the dark pool cast by the canopy
in the oval shade under the tree

to be chalk, where sun lights up grass
in a blaze of reflective green glass
that may yellow to blond and fade
unless in this oval of shade

to live with sheep under a tree
where a hollow stem houses a bee
and the hookety rooks catch light
in glistenings of daylit night

to sleep and then gather a seed,
seed of a thought, thought of a seed
in the oval shade under the tree
in the dark grass under the canopy

to look up through the sieve of the tree
at wind rushing leaves like the sea
to live with the clouds of sheep
in the woolly birdstrutting heap

to seek like a picketty beak,
to nod with the hook of a rook
whose shadowflights unsettle
the trembling thistle, the trembling nettle

to write in the shade of this tree
against the dark of the canopy

# Steven O'Brien

## *Highdown*

Know that I was golden then
Alone on the lip of the hillfort
Above Goring,
With the after-blaze of a July day on my skin.

Night was something to be hurdled,
A colt joy of running blind,
In the leaf-shuddering twitten.

Up there the wind blew through me,
A ripe blackberry tremor.
Felt like it might stain me dark,
As I fell into the grass
And the thorn trees all stood one legged
On the slope behind the ramparts.

I had no reckoning
Of the ancient spikes
Once stowed in the white clunch —

Bone prick pins.
Charm-fasteners.

A bronze dagger
Secret, furtive and winter green.
This one had been set point upwards
In the grave.

A fierce black angon spear,
Dread belly barb.
Never to be withdrawn, once thrust.

All these have been dug from their long hoarding
And numbered in the buff boxes
Of county vaults.

I was in my colt years,
With giddy eyes and amber limbs,
And doused in moonlight I lay awake
On the shallow turf
Until the dog star rose.

Yet often I climb out of a dream
That has put me back up on that hill
With a wet blade turning in my guts,

For I know well now that it is
Bitter, curse-sown ground.
Bones of surly men have also been taken,
From the white pits
Along with their rust-flaking weaponry,
But many lie there still,
Unexhumed,
Hunched among the flints,

And all through the darkness
They were watching me in the coils of brambles
And nettle banks.

In middle age I would not go there
At night,
Alone.

# *Wild Hunt*

On Cleggan strand
That lean chaser of a morning
Under a fast breaking lintel
Of grey sky.

The raw shore.
The chieftain's empty chamber
And you dancing.

Your coat bluster-hooked
And the nape of your neck
Like smooth shell
Given for an instant
In the eye
Between flap and rain.

The gold of your hair
Plaiting the wind's tail.

And me
Caught in the slipstream
Of your wild laughter.

Then the gale tearing itself

Into a pack of sleek wish-hounds,
Coursing through the cromlech frame
With split sunlight on their heels

While still you spun
Funnelled in the gap
Amid the glee and yelp
Of the glancing storm shucks —

Your hood flung back
And your hair
Now a glistening torc
On your white throat,

Arms spread and lifted —
A joy wrack huntress.

# *Zither Child*

*For Flossie*

i

Of all things a zither!

I was astonished
By its pylon saw and jingle
When she tugged it
From the trinket-midden.

Time withers at her door jamb.
And her decree is chaos
Over cups, bangles and scarves —
Every filched bauble
Piled and trodden in.

ii

When she flung a tune
Each of her fingers was cat's paw
Plucking crazy feathers
From blond wood
And wire —

A Zingari wedding reel
Heard in a subway.
Ribbon music and mischief
Riddling up an escalator.

Beads of mountain rain,
Shoal flickers,
Strung
On her flat and cunning
Harp.

iii

Arc now
To point-forged water

Hammer stone chink
In the Doo Lough Pass —

And her poise
In the peeling wind,

Like she has leaped freshly tempered
From an under bridge smithy —

Her salmon flanked legs
Sloughing silver scales.

Each splashed glede
A zinc note

As she jumps trimly
The shutters of the sun.

# Colette Sensier

## Get Thee Glass Eyes

A man is being scratched out of the hills
- no, a man is *in the course of being* scratched out of the hills.
They are going to scratch a man out of the hills.

When the vague teetering of opposite cliffs
seen through cloudless weather, when you peer,
is only theoretical and unbound –

the chalk man under the cliffs remains,
milking the milk of the earth's old eyes.

Sure, sturdy, surely there. They fiddle for him
with careful silver tools and awkward speeches.

The air smells special today. I whirl my stick in the pool
and stab it back into the ground
like I was mad, and the ground, eyes.

# *In the Weald*

Daisies unwind their yellow circles,
spires and spheres counting out the hours
the country mice are killing, after school.

We've stashed the bottles of wine and beer
to dampen in the trees' arm muscles
flexing below the water level,

their labels shivering verbal echoes
beneath the double view of glass and water.
Once a sheep died in this river,

her four feet in the air. Now the fields
with their continuing animal life
stretch out before us. We watch the bone-white sky,

the frogs, each other; the boys joke, drink, wrestle
on blunted throats of flattened grass.
No deadlines yet and no reason,

when we turned as a pack and ran
against the pale wheat, our t shirts and bikini tops
the purest colours in fields of change and shade.

No time for rain creeping over the bottles,
the sky, the river, the corpse of the forgotten sheep,
and our feet, running away from the woods

# Marguerite

*Effeuiller la marguerite.* Strip off the florets
like sessile hairs swelling bulbous roots
under the scalp and coming out in handfuls.

The strong yellow sphere is breathing for you
through millions of hidden nostrils.

From every direction, they tell bees what to do,
*effeuille-moi,* love me or love me not.

My parents looked over the ocean
and turned great-grandmother Daisy into me, Marguerite.
Marguerites grow in our garden — the dog-daisy,
the ox-eye, the moon — junky and mixed
as new words in a child's mouth.

Let me unfold you,
let me tear you down from the wall like a creeper,
its thin shoots spreading like a wealth of Catholic children.

The flower grows so vulgar,
its names shift through the past remembered
as peeled-off petals, a weighted burst of pollen.

# Biographies

**Hannah Brockbank** has an MA in Creative Writing from the University of Chichester. Recent publications featuring her work include *Hallelujah for 50ft Women* (Bloodaxe 2015), *The London Magazine* and *Envoi*. Her first pamphlet, *Bloodlines*, is due for publication in 2017 by Indigo Dreams Publishing.

**Lydia Fulleylove** has published two collections, *Notes on Sea and Land* (Happen*Stance* 2011) and *Estuary* (Two Ravens Press 2014). Her poem 'Night Drive' was shortlisted for the Forward Prize in 2010. She has led many community arts projects.

**Kate Miller** grew up in Hampshire, studied at Cambridge and London, and became a writer. Her book *The Observances* (Carcanet 2015) was shortlisted for the 2015 Costa Book Award and for the Seamus Heaney Centre Poetry Prize.

**Zoe Mitchell** lives and works on the South Coast. She has been published in national poetry magazines *The Rialto*, *Brittle Star* and *The Cannon's Mouth*, and has recently completed an MA in Creative Writing at the University of Chichester.

**Stephanie Norgate** is a poet and playwright. Her collections are *Hidden River* (Bloodaxe 2008, Forward and Jerwood Aldeburgh First Collection prize shortlists) and *The Blue Den* (Bloodaxe 2012). Her plays have been broadcast on BBC R4. She is a Reader in Creative Writing at the University of Chichester and a freelance poet.

**Steven O'Brien** is a widely published poet, with two collections: *Dark Hill Dreams* (Agenda 2006) and *Scrying Stone* (Greenwich Exchange 2010). He is a novelist, academic and editor of *The London Magazine*. He is currently working on *Britannic Myths*, a series of creative prose retellings in collaboration with artist Joe Machine.

**Colette Sensier** is a poetry, prose and drama writer from Brighton. She's been featured in the *Salt Book of Younger Poets* and other anthologies and magazines. Her debut collection is *Skinless* (Eyewear 2012).